THE AGE OF EXPLORATION

ENZO GEORGE

Cavendish
Square
New York

Published in 2017 by Cavendish Square Publishing, LLC
243 5th Avenue, Suite 136 New York, NY 10016

Website: cavendishsq.com

This publication represents the opinions and views of the author based on his or her personal experiences, knowledge, and research. The information in this book serves as a general guide only. The author and publisher have used their best efforts in preparing this book and disclaim liabilty rising directly or indirectly for the use and application of this book.

CPSIA compliance information: Batch #CS16CSQ.

All websites were available and accurate when this book went to press.

Library of Congress Cataloging-in-Publication Data

Names: George, Enzo.
Title: The age of exploration / Enzo George.
Description: New York : Cavendish Square, 2017. | Series: Primary sources in world history | Includes index.
Identifiers: ISBN 9781502618146 (library bound) | ISBN 9781502618153 (ebook)
Subjects: LCSH: Discoveries in geography—History—15th century—Juvenile literature. |
Discoveries in geography—History—16th century—Juvenile literature. | Explorers—Juvenile literature.
Classification: LCC G82.G47 2017 | DDC 910'.9'024—dc23

For Brown Bear Books Ltd:
Editorial Director: Lindsey Lowe
Managing Editor: Tim Cooke
Children's Publisher: Anne O'Daly
Design Manager: Keith Davis
Designer: Lynne Lennon
Picture Manager: Sophie Mortimer

Printed in the United States of America

CONTENTS

INTRODUCTION

Primary sources are the best way to get close to people from the past. They include the things people wrote in diaries, letters, or books; the paintings, drawings, maps, or cartoons they created; and even the buildings they constructed, the clothes they wore, or the objects they owned. Such sources often reveal a lot about how people saw themselves and how they thought about their world.

This book collects a range of primary sources from a period in history that stretched from about 1400 to about 1800. During this time, explorers and other travelers visited many parts of the globe and encountered other cultures. European nations, in particular, sent many explorers around the world.

In Europe, this period is sometimes called "the Age of Exploration." Improved shipbuilding and navigational tools allowed explorers such as Christopher Columbus to reach the Americas, Vasco da Gama to sail to India, and Ferdinand Magellan to circumnavigate the globe. Their encounters with peoples in the "New World," Asia, and the Pacific would have lasting consequences. Meanwhile, states such as China sent out their own expeditions of exploration. By the end of the 1700s, even remote parts of the world were connected by networks of trade and political power.

HOW TO USE THIS BOOK

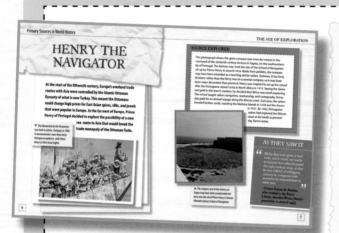

Each spread contains at least one primary source. Look out for "Source Explored" boxes that explain images from the age of exploration and who made them and why. There are also "As They Saw It" boxes that contain quotes from people of the period.

Some boxes contain more detailed information about a particular aspect of a subject. The subjects are arranged in roughly chronological order. They focus on key events or people. There is a full timeline of the period at the back of the book.

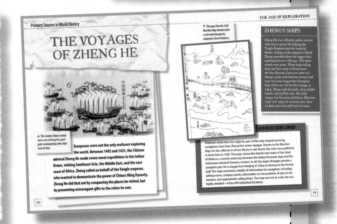

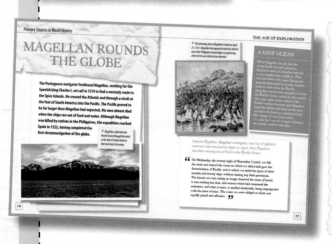

Some spreads feature a longer extract from a contemporary eyewitness. Look for the colored introduction that explains who the writer is and the origin of his or her account. These accounts are often accompanied by a related visual primary source.

HENRY THE NAVIGATOR

At the start of the fifteenth century, Europe's overland trade routes with Asia were controlled by the Islamic Ottoman Dynasty of what is now Turkey. This meant the Ottomans could charge high prices for East Asian spices, silks, and jewels that were popular in Europe. In the far west of Europe, Prince Henry of Portugal decided to explore the possibility of a new sea route to Asia that would break the trade monopoly of the Ottoman Turks.

▼ *The Monument to the Discoveries was built in Lisbon, Portugal, in 1960. It commemorates more than thirty Portuguese explorers, with Prince Henry at their head (right).*

SOURCE EXPLORED

This photograph shows the giant compass rose (*rosa dos ventos*) in the courtyard of the sixteenth century fortress in Sagres, on the southwestern tip of Portugal. The fortress may mark the site of the School of Navigation set up by Prince Henry in around 1416. Made from pebbles, the compass may have been intended as a teaching aid for sailors. However, it has forty divisions rather than the thirty-two on a normal compass, so it may have been more decorative than practical. Henry was inspired to set up the school after the Portuguese seized Ceuta in North Africa in 1415. Seeing the slaves and gold in the town's markets, he decided that Africa was worth exploring. The school taught sailors navigation, seamanship, and cartography. Henry also paid for an annual voyage along the African coast. Each year, the sailors traveled farther south, reaching the Madeira Islands in 1418 and the Azores in 1431. By 1462, Portuguese sailors had explored the African coast as far south as present-day Sierra Leone.

▲ *The compass rose in the fortress at Sagres may have been created while the town was the site of Prince Henry's famous fifteenth-century School of Navigation.*

AS THEY SAW IT

“ All his days were spent in hard work, and it would not readily be believed how often he passed the night without sleep, so that by dint [effort] of unflagging industry he conquered what seemed to be impossibilities to other men. ”

—Gomes Eannes de Azurara, who worked in the Royal Library, describes Prince Henry's personality in around 1453.

TECHNOLOGICAL BACKGROUND

When Prince Henry of Portugal started his school of navigation in the early fifteenth century, seamanship was not very developed. Ships' navigators relied largely on guesswork and what they could see around them to work out where they were. For that reason they often stayed close to coastlines. With Henry's backing, Portuguese sailors helped develop new instruments for navigation and new ocean-going ships. The new ships and equipment enabled sailors to travel farther than ever before.

◀ The caravel was light and fast, but it was also strong and stable. This made it ideal for sailing in heavy seas. It carried a crew of around twenty-five.

▼ *This astrolabe was made in Persia early in the Middle Ages. The rotating arms allowed sailors to line up their position with those of heavenly objects.*

AS THEY SAW IT

" In the year 1484, King John of Portugal fitted out two caravels, well provided with men, provisions and munitions of war for three years, and he ordered ... they should proceed southward and eastward as far as they possibly could.... We also took all sorts of spices to show the natives what we went in search of.... "

—Written on the world's oldest surviving globe by the Portuguese sailor Martin Behaim in 1492.

SOURCE EXPLORED

The astrolabe was invented in Arabia and reached Europe in the tenth century. It enabled navigators to measure the angle of heavenly bodies such as the sun or moon above the horizon. This allowed sailors to work out their latitude, or how far north or south their ship was. The cross-staff and quadrant were other navigational tools that helped sailors measure the height of heavenly bodies in order to plot their position at sea. Another instrument that helped to improve navigation in the fifteenth century was the magnetic compass. Invented in China in the second century BCE, the compass reached Europe in the thirteenth century. Its magnetized needle always points north, which allowed sailors to orient themselves when there were no visible landmarks. Meanwhile, advances in shipbuilding also allowed the Portuguese to sail farther from land. The caravel was lighter than earlier ships but it was also very stable, so it was well suited for sailing on the open ocean. Its triangular lateen sails allowed it to sail into the wind.

THE VOYAGES OF ZHENG HE

▲ *This modern Chinese stamp shows one of Zheng He's giant junks surrounded by other ships from his fleet.*

Europeans were not the only seafarers exploring the world. Between 1405 and 1433, the Chinese admiral Zheng He made seven naval expeditions in the Indian Ocean, visiting Southeast Asia, the Middle East, and the east coast of Africa. Zheng sailed on behalf of the Yongle emperor, who wanted to demonstrate the power of China's Ming Dynasty. Zheng He did that not by conquering the places he visited, but by presenting extravagant gifts to the rulers he met.

▼ *This page from the 1628 Mao Kun Map showed sailors a safe route through the dangerous Strait of Malacca.*

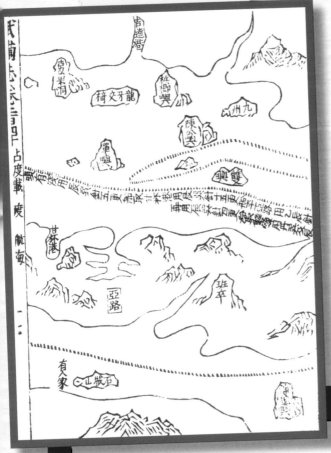

ZHENG'S SHIPS

Zheng He was a Muslim palace servant who rose to power by helping the Yongle Emperor gain the imperial throne. Sailing on the emperor's behalf, Zheng assembled fleets far bigger than anything known in Europe. The main vessels were junks. These large sailing ships had been used in China since the Han Dynasty (220 BCE–200 CE). Zheng's junks each had four storeys and were ten times longer than European ships of the era. On his first voyage in 1405, Zheng took 62 junks, 225 smaller vessels, and 27,800 men. His final voyage was his most ambitious. Between 1431 and 1433, he covered more than 12,600 miles (20,278 km) of ocean.

SOURCE EXPLORED

Historians think that this might be part of the only original surviving navigation chart from Zheng He's seven voyages. Known as the *Mao Kun Map*, for the collector in whose library it was found, the chart was published in book form in 1628. This page shows the islands and coasts of the Strait of Malacca, a narrow waterway between the Malay Peninsula (top) and the Indonesian island of Sumatra (center). In all, the map's 40 pages provide a complete plan for a voyage from Nanjing in China to Hormuz in the Persian Gulf. The map contained a wealth of information for navigators: including sailing routes, compass points, information on the positions of stars in the heavens, and approximate sailing times. The map was not to scale, but was highly detailed—it lists 499 individual locations.

CHRISTOPHER COLUMBUS

The Italian navigator Christopher Columbus believed there must be a westerly trade route across the Atlantic Ocean to East Asia. King Ferdinand and Queen Isabella of Spain agreed to fund Columbus's expedition. They hoped to benefit from the spice trade. Columbus landed on a Bahamian island in the Caribbean on October 12, 1492. He was convinced he had reached the East Indies rather than the Americas.

▼ This later painting shows Columbus leaving Palos in Spain on his first voyage. Columbus made three more voyages to the Americas between 1492 and 1503.

Columbus' journal entry for October 12, 1492, describes how land was spotted and how the Spaniards went ashore:

"" At two o'clock in the morning the land was discovered, at two leagues' distance; they took in sail and remained under the square-sail lying to [stationary] till day, which was Friday, when they found themselves near a small island, one of the Lucayos, called in the Indian language Guanahani. Presently they descried [saw] people, naked, and the Admiral [Columbus] landed in the boat, which was armed, along with Martin Alonzo Pinzon, and Vincent Yanez his brother, captain of the *Nina*. The Admiral bore the royal standard, and the two captains each a banner of the Green Cross... Arrived on shore, they saw trees very green, many streams of water, and diverse sorts of fruits. ""

◀ Armed soldiers guard Columbus as he makes his first contact with the Taíno of Hispaniola. Within a century the Taíno were largely wiped out by the effects of disease and slavery.

SOURCE EXPLORED

This engraving from 1592 shows Columbus meeting Taíno Natives on the island of Hispaniola (now the Dominican Republic–Haiti) on December 6, 1492. The Taíno offer Columbus gifts, while sailors raise a cross in the background. Columbus founded a settlement on Hispaniola, which he hoped had rich resources, such as spices or gold. He also wanted to persuade the Taíno to follow Christianity rather than their traditional religion. However, he ended up forcing the Taíno and other Native peoples into slavery and treated them with brutality.

VASCO DA GAMA

The Portuguese explorer Vasco da Gama was the first navigator to sail from Europe to India. He had studied the expeditions of earlier explorers and believed he could find a sea route to the east. Leaving Portugal in 1497 he sailed down the west coast of Africa and around its southern tip, the Cape of Good Hope, into the Indian Ocean. He reached Calicut (now Kozhikode) on the Indian coast on May 20, 1498.

▼ *The Cape of Good Hope is near the southernmost tip of Africa. Da Gama rounded the cape on November 22, 1497, and sailed into the Indian Ocean.*

SOURCE EXPLORED

This illustration of some of da Gama's ships comes from a map of his expedition to India in 1497. Da Gama left Portugal with four ships and 170 men. Two years later, only two ships and 55 men returned. Many sailors had died from disease on the return voyage across the Indian Ocean. However, da Gama also brought back a valuable cargo of spices. The overland spice trade with Asia had been controlled by the Muslim Ottomans in Turkey. The seaborne trade route through the Red Sea and Egypt to the Mediterranean was controlled by the Republic of Venice. Now da Gama had found a direct sea route from Europe to Asia, the Portuguese had their own access to the spices of Asia. After his voyage, the Portuguese sent a large fleet to India every year to trade for valuable spices.

▲ This illustration shows three of Vasco da Gama's ships at sea. Da Gama sailed in the São Gabriel (center). His brother, Paulo, commanded the São Raphael (top).

MONSOON WINDS

The Indian Ocean experiences seasonal winds known as monsoons. The winds blow regularly in one direction, then the other. They are easy to predict, so local sailors always traveled with the monsoon winds to make crossing the ocean quicker. When Vasco da Gama left India on August 29, 1498, however, he ignored local advice that the monsoon winds were about to change direction. As a result, the voyage across the Indian Ocean took his two remaining ships 132 days (the outward journey had taken just 23 days). By the time the ships reached land, half the men had died from starvation or diseases such as scurvy.

MAGELLAN ROUNDS THE GLOBE

The Portuguese navigator Ferdinand Magellan, working for the Spanish king Charles I, set sail in 1519 to find a westerly route to the Spice Islands. He crossed the Atlantic and through a strait at the foot of South America into the Pacific. The Pacific proved to be far larger than Magellan had expected. His men almost died when the ships ran out of food and water. Although Magellan was killed by natives in the Philippines, the expedition reached Spain in 1522, having completed the first circumnavigation of the globe.

▼ *Magellan sailed into the Pacific Ocean through the strait at the foot of South America that now bears his name.*

▼ *This drawing shows Magellan's death on April 27, 1521. Magellan had agreed to help the chief of one of the Philippine islands fight a neighboring chief, but he was killed in the skirmish.*

A VAST OCEAN

When Magellan set sail, the size of the Earth was still unknown. Explorers such as Columbus believed it was smaller than it really is. That was one reason why many Europeans believed there must be an easy western route to Asia across the Pacific. Magellan was the first navigator to cross the Pacific Ocean, which he also named. The vast ocean covers a third of the Earth's surface, however, and Magellan sailed for almost 100 days on the open sea before he found an inhabited island. His voyage of over 7,000 miles (11,265 km) was the longest unbroken sea journey made to that date.

Antonio Pigafetta, Magellan's navigator, was one of eighteen survivors who returned to Spain in 1522. Here Pigafetta describes running out of food in the Pacific Ocean:

❝ On Wednesday, the twenty-eight of November (1520), we left the strait and entered the ocean to which we afterwards gave the denomination of Pacific, and in which we sailed the space of three months and twenty days, without tasting any fresh provisions. The biscuit we were eating no longer deserved the name of bread; it was nothing but dust, and worms which had consumed the substance, and what is more, it smelled intolerably, being impregnated with the urine of mice. The water we were obliged to drink was equally putrid and offensive. ❞

MUGHAL INDIA

The Taj Mahal was built by the Mughal emperor Shah Jahan in memory of his wife, Mumtaz Mahal. Completed in 1653, it was one of the high points of Islamic architecture in India.

When Vasco da Gama arrived in Calicut (Kozhikode) in 1498, the Indians were unimpressed by the cloth and other goods he brought as presents. India was home to its own wealthy and technologically advanced kingdoms. While Calicut and other parts of southern India were in the hands of Hindu princes, from 1526 northern Indian was dominated by the Islamic Mughal Empire. The splendor of the Mughal court outstripped anything known in the West. Its court was famous for its sophistication throughout the world.

Sir Thomas Roe was sent as an English ambassador to the Mughal court in India. Here he records his visit to the Emperor Jahangir in January 1616:

❝ I went at four in the evening to the *durbar*, which is the place where the Moghul sits out daily, to entertain strangers, to receive petitions and presents, to give commands, to see and be seen.... He comes every morning to a window ... and shows himself to the common people. At noon he returns there and sits some hours to see the fight of elephants and wild beasts ... from whence he retires to sleep. At afternoon, he returns to the durbar before mentioned. At eight, after supper, he comes down to a court where is a throne of stone wherein he sits ... to which none are admitted but of great quality, and few of those without leave; where he discourses on all matters with great affability. ❞

▲ This miniature painting shows Shah Jahan sitting on the Peacock Throne of the Mughals. The jeweled throne was kept in the Red Fort of Delhi.

MUGHAL EMPIRE

The Mughal Empire in India began in 1526, when the Central Asian ruler Babur defeated the sultan of Delhi in battle and seized the throne. Babur and his successors of the Timurid dynasty ruled much of India until the British removed the last emperor in 1858. The most famous Mughal, Akbar, ruled from 1556 to 1605. He expanded the empire through warfare and married a Hindu princess, which helped to promote religious tolerance between India's Hindus and Muslims. The empire reached its greatest extent in 1707, before European powers began to take more control of regions of India.

MERCATOR'S BREAKTHROUGH

As European seafarers explored the globe, cartographers mapped their discoveries. It remained difficult, however, to create maps and charts that could be used for navigation, because any representation of the spherical Earth on a flat piece of paper was distorted. In 1569, the Flemish-born cartographer Gerardus Mercator came up with a new projection, or way to represent the Earth, that allowed sailors to plot their course using straight lines on a flat map. No one really knows how Mercator figured out the math behind his breakthrough map.

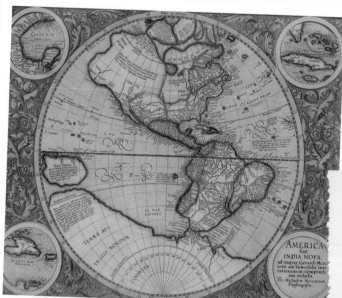

◀ This late fifteenth-century map reflects the growing geographical knowledge of Europeans. It shows North and South America, but also a huge imaginary southern continent.

As early as **1546**, Mercator wrote a letter to his friend, Antoine **Perronet**, explaining how he thought he might solve the problem of representing the round Earth on flat paper:

> " I had to wonder, how it could be that ship-courses, when the distances of the places were exactly measured, at times show their difference of latitude [position north or south of the Equator] greater than it really is, and at other times on the contrary, smaller, and again frequently upon a correct difference of latitude for the places in question. Since this matter caused me anxiety for a long time, because I saw that all nautical charts, by which I was hoping especially to correct geographical errors, would not serve their purpose, I began to investigate carefully the cause of their errors, and found them chiefly to rest on an ignorance of the nature of the magnet [compass]. "

▶ *Many sailors found Mercator's map too complex to understand, and it caught on only slowly.*

SOURCE EXPLORED

This is the 1569 map that Mercator devised to help sailors navigate. To allow them to plot their courses in straight lines, he gave the continents the right shapes but the wrong sizes. On the map, for example, Africa does not appear to be much larger than Greenland. In fact, it is fourteen times bigger. This distortion meant Mercator's map gave more accurate information about latitude than earlier maps. The Mercator projection is still the most common map projection today, but it has been criticized for making the wealthier nations of the Northern Hemisphere appear larger and thus more important than parts of Africa, southern Asia, and South America.

EXPLORING SIBERIA

In Russia, Emperor Ivan IV, known as Ivan the Terrible, encouraged exploration eastward, into the vast region of Siberia. The first explorer of Siberia was the Cossack Yermak Timofeyevich. In 1581, Yermak and his men traveled east of the Ural Mountains, returning to Russia with many valuable furs. Russia used Siberia as a source of fur until the late eighteenth century. It sold the fur in Europe and Asia.

▼ *Much of Siberia is uninhabited wilderness that suffers from severe weather during winter. It is a difficult environment for humans to survive in.*

◀ *Russian settlement of much of Siberia was limited to well-defended military positions like this one.*

SOURCE EXPLORED

This Chinese map shows a Russian military camp in eastern Siberia in the late seventeenth century. The explorer Yermak Timofeyevich was killed in mysterious circumstances in 1585 during Russian military expansion into Siberia. He is said to have been murdered by the head of a local tribe. However, the expansion he had begun led to the Russians reaching the Pacific Ocean in 1639. Their influence spread across the whole of Asia. Today Siberia remains part of Russia. It is a sparsely populated region that stretches from the Ural Mountains in the west to the Pacific Ocean in the east and from the Arctic Ocean south toward Kazakhstan and the Mongolian and Chinese northern borders. Yermak's pivotal role in making the breakthrough to Siberia made him a folk hero in Russia.

THE FUR TRADE

For much of ancient history, furs were the easiest way to keep warm in poorly heated homes, either as clothing or as blankets. Furs were also a luxury. While the poor wore furs such as rabbit or squirrel, the wealthy paid for softer or more attractively colored furs. One of the most prized furs in Europe was white ermine, made from a stoat found in Siberia. The Russian seizure of Siberia allowed it to dominate the European fur trade for centuries. In the late eighteenth century, however, the trade was taken over by French and British merchants who trapped fur animals such as beaver in North America. Beaver pelt was treated to make it smooth and shiny and it was then used to make hats.

THE SPICE ISLANDS

▲ Spices were valuable in Europe, where they helped to disguise the taste of food that was stale or that lacked in flavor. Most originated from south and Southeast Asia.

One of the most prized cargoes for European explorers in Asia was spices, such as nutmeg, cloves, pepper, and mace. The spices gave flavor to food and were also used in medicines. Most spices grew on the Spice Islands of Indonesia, known as the Moluccas or Malaku Islands. The Portuguese arrived in 1513 and took control of the spice trade. From the mid-1500s they were challenged by the Spaniards and the Dutch. From 1599, the Dutch gradually established a monopoly over the trade.

This map of the East Indies (now Indonesia) shows a confusing cluster of islands. In the early eighteenth century, Dutch explorers in particular contributed to far more accurate European knowledge of the region.

SOURCE EXPLORED

This is a 1683 version of a map of what is now Indonesia drawn two decades earlier by the French cartographer Nicolas Sanson, based on reports by European navigators. Although trade with the Spice Islands was well established, the map is not geographically accurate. The trade was important because it offered huge profits. Spices were sold in Europe for anything between 1,000 and 60,000 percent profit. The Portuguese, Spanish, and Dutch competed to control the trade in the sixteenth century. The English tried to set up a link with the islands. In 1616, an expedition led by Nathaniel Courthope set up a base on Run, a small island in the Moluccas, to challenge Dutch control of the nutmeg trade, but his fort was besieged by the Dutch for three years. After Courthope was killed in 1620, the English withdrew.

AS THEY SAW IT

" Every year ... on the beach, large heaps like haystacks are burned. The fire sometimes burns for eight days. As long as it lasts, sentries stand there day and night, so that nobody can take anything. The oil flows to the sea like a sizable stream. The Chinese have often wanted to buy the soil where the nuts were burned from the Noble Company, but were not able to obtain it. "

—Dutch merchant Ernst Christoph Barchewitz describes burning nutmeg in 1730 to cause a shortage in Europe that would keep prices high.

THE DUTCH EAST INDIA COMPANY

▲ A replica of a Dutch East India Company trading ship from the seventeenth century is preserved today next to the old company headquarters in Amsterdam in the Netherlands.

In 1602 the Dutch set up the Vereenigde Oost-Indische Compagnie (VOC, or Dutch East India Company) to control trade with the Spice Islands. The company rose to dominate global commerce for nearly two hundred years before it was dissolved in 1799. The VOC became hugely powerful. It set up its own colony in what is now Indonesia where it operated as a government. The VOC was able to wage war on local rulers if necessary, had its own army, and produced its own coinage.

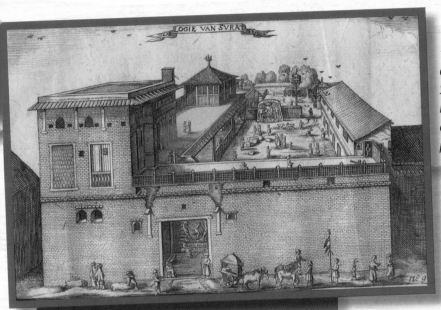

SOURCE EXPLORED

The Dutch cloth merchant Pieter van den Broecke made this engraving in April 1629, while he was working for the VOC. His picture shows an East India Company warehouse and accommodation in the Indian city of Surat. The spice trade was still centered on the Spice Islands, where the VOC set up its capital at Batavia (now Jakarta). However, the VOC soon expanded its operations more widely in Asia. It began to trade in India in 1604, mainly to acquire silks and cotton. It built "factories" like this along the coast, where stores could be gathered ready to be loaded onto ships. The VOC also had a monopoly on European trade with Japan, where it traded goods such as gold, silver, and porcelain.

SAILING TO ASIA

After the establishment of the VOC, two or three large Dutch fleets sailed to Asia each year. The Dutch built special, larger ships to carry more passengers and cargo. The ships carried cannon and ammunition to defend themselves if necessary. Between 1602 and 1610, 8,500 people sailed to Asia. They were mainly merchants. Soon about 4,000 people were making the voyage each year. It took about eight months to reach the Spice Islands, and conditions on the ships were crowded and unhygienic. When the Dutch arrived in Asia, they lived in well-defended factories where they stored the goods they traded.

MATTEO RICCI

Matteo Ricci was an Italian-born Jesuit priest. He introduced Christianity to China, where he lived for over thirty years. Ricci served as a missionary in the Dutch colony of Macau, where he learned Chinese and studied local customs. In 1583 Ricci was invited to China by a local governor who had heard of his skill as a cartographer and mathematician. In 1601 the Wanli Emperor invited Ricci to Beijing, where Ricci set up a Catholic church. He also introduced the Chinese to European scientific advances.

▼ *The world map Matteo Ricci produced in 1602 was the first map in China to show the Americas. It included descriptions of the continents and praise for the Chinese emperor.*

▼ Although Ricci's mastery of cartography and Western technology won him respect in the imperial court, he never met the Chinese emperor.

SOURCE EXPLORED

This engraving of Matteo Ricci (left) and the Chinese mathematician Xu Guangqi appeared in a book by Athanasius Kircher in 1667. The two friends worked together translating texts from and into Chinese. Xu Guangqi was a senior official within the court of the Wanli Emperor. He converted to Catholicism and became one of the so-called "Three Pillars" of the early Catholic Church in China. Among the works he and Ricci translated was *Elements of Geometry*, by the ancient Greek mathematician Euclid. The book appeared in 1607 and introduced the Chinese to important ideas of Western logic and mathematics. Ricci was also celebrated for creating a world map based on Western exploration. As advisor to the imperial court from 1601, he was the first foreigner to be admitted to the Forbidden City, the imperial complex at the heart of Beijing.

EUROPE AND ASIA

▲ The Chinese House was built in the gardens of Potsdam Palace in Germany from 1755 to 1764 on the orders of King Frederick the Great of Prussia.

As trade with East Asia increased in the late seventeenth and eighteenth centuries, a great fashion arose in Europe not only for Chinese and Japanese goods but also for the styles associated with Asian art. This fashion, known as Chinoiserie, was highly decorative, in contrast with the symmetry and order of the visual traditions of the Renaissance. European artists set out to reflect East Asian styles in everything from architecture and painting to ceramics and garden design.

SOURCE EXPLORED

One of the most highly sought-after and influential imports from Asia was Chinese porcelain. This vase dates from the Ming Dynasty (1368–1644). Porcelain, a form of very fine clay china, had been developed under the Mongol Yuan Dynasty in the thirteenth and fourteenth centuries, but it was Ming craftspeople who perfected the technique of making and glazing porcelain. This vase was created between 1425 and 1436, based on the shape of an ancient bronze vessel. Like much Ming porcelain, it is finished in a distinctive cobalt-blue glaze. Europeans coveted Chinese porcelain and tried to produce it themselves. They only succeeded in 1708, when porcelain that could be fired at very high temperatures was developed in Meissen in Germany.

▲ The cobalt-blue glaze that is typical of Ming Dynasty China was introduced during the rule of the Xuande Emperor in the early fifteenth century.

CHINESE SILK

The Chinese learned how to harvest thread from silk worms as long ago as 2700 BCE. The Europeans stole silk worms from China and began their own silk industry in the sixth century CE, but Chinese silk remained highly valued. During the thirteenth and fourteenth centuries, a network of trade routes grew up connecting China to the West across Asia. The network was known as the Silk Road, because silk was one of most important goods to pass along it. The route's importance declined with the opening of new sea routes to Asia.

THE SLAVE TRADE

From the middle of the fifteenth century, European traders began to ship black Africans to Europe as slaves. In the sixteenth century, slaves were shipped to European colonies in the Caribbean and North America. The trade reached its peak in the eighteenth century, when millions of African slaves were sent to work on sugar, cotton, and tobacco plantations in the Americas. Estimates suggest up to ten million Africans were forced from home to work in the New World.

▼ *In this colored version of an engraving from 1853, a female slave is sold at an auction in Richmond, Virginia.*

SOURCE EXPLORED

In this illustration from 1859, bound slaves are marched by slave traders through the African interior. Slaves were captured all over Africa, often by other African peoples, and marched to the West African coast. There they were sold to European traders in some thirty slave forts along a 2,000-mile-long (3,200 km) coast. The slaves were held in dirty, crowded conditions until they were loaded onto ships to be taken across the Atlantic. The conditions on the ships were usually even worse. The slaves were held beneath the deck.

▲ Slaves are marched toward the African coast fastened together in a coffle, or line.

Alexander Falconbridge served as a surgeon on several slave ships. He came to oppose the trade in his 1788 account, *An Account of the Slave Trade on the Coast of Africa*:

❝ As soon as the wretched Africans, purchased at the fairs, fall into the hands of the black traders, they experience an earnest [a taste] of those dreadful sufferings which they are doomed in future to undergo.... They are brought from the places where they are purchased ... in canoes; at the bottom of which they lie, having their hands tied, and a strict watch is kept over them. Their usage in other respects, during the time of the passage, which generally lasts several days, is equally cruel. Their allowance of food is so scanty, that it is barely sufficient to support nature. They are, besides, much exposed to the violent rains which frequently fall here, being covered only with mats that afford but a slight defense; and as there is usually water at the bottom of the canoes, from their leaking, they are scarcely ever dry. ❞

33

PLANTATIONS IN THE CARIBBEAN

▲ *In this nineteenth-century illustration of a sugar plantation in Cuba, the slaves' huts are to the left, the owner's house in the center, and the sugar mill on the right.*

The first African slaves were brought to the Caribbean by the Spanish in about 1510. From the 1520s, Europeans developed a taste for sugar, and sugar plantations spread throughout the Caribbean. English, Spanish, and Portuguese merchants shipped African slaves to the Caribbean to grow sugar cane and operate the mills that extracted the sugar. Such work was labor intensive, but using free labor from slaves made the sugar industry a highly profitable one.

Olaudah Equiano was kidnapped from Nigeria as a child and shipped to a plantation in Barbados. Eventually, he bought his freedom and moved to Europe, where he described his experiences in his autobiography in 1789:

> **"** Another negro man was half hanged, and then burnt, for attempting to poison a cruel overseer.... These overseers are indeed for the most part persons of the worst character of any denomination of men in the West Indies. Unfortunately, many humane gentlemen, by not residing on their estates, are obliged to leave the management of them in the hands of these human butchers, who cut and mangle the slaves in a shocking manner on the most trifling occasions, and altogether treat them in every respect like brutes. **"**

◄ Theodor de Bry's engraving of sugar production is an idealized view of a process that was in fact hard, dirty labor, with the threat of injury from sharp sugar cane, heavy millstones, or boiling sugar.

SOURCE EXPLORED

By the sixteenth century, it was common for slaves to process sugar on large plantations in the Caribbean. The Belgian engraver and mapmaker Theodor de Bry produced this detailed image of sugar production in 1595, without ever having seen the process. The raw cane was cut from the fields (*top right*), then crushed beneath huge millstones (*top left*) to release the sap. The sugar was boiled to create crystals (*bottom left*), then poured into pots to allow any remaining syrup to drip out (*bottom center*). The process was labor intensive, as were cotton and tobacco cultivation. As plantations spread, Caribbean islands such as Nevis saw their African population grow from 20 percent in the 1650s to almost 80 percent by the early eighteenth century.

THE GOLDEN AGE OF PIRACY

As colonies spread around the world, pirates began to attack ships sailing to and from Europe. The period from 1680 to 1720 was a "golden age" for pirates. There were few legal forces in places such as the Caribbean, so pirates could easily steal gold, silver, and other cargoes. Some attacked foreign ships on behalf of their own governments. These pirates were known as privateers.

▼ This seventeenth-century Dutch painting shows an English naval vessel (left) under attack from pirate ships in the Mediterranean Sea.

SOURCE EXPLORED

This engraving from 1724 shows the most famous of all pirates, the Englishman Edward Teach, better known as Blackbeard. The pirate brandishes his sword and wears six pistols in a belt across his chest. Smoking fuses burn beneath his hat to increase his terrifying appearance. Blackbeard operated off the coasts of Virginia and the Carolinas and throughout the Caribbean in his forty-gun ship, the *Queen Anne's Revenge*. In May 1718 he blockaded the harbor at Charleston, South Carolina, stealing from ships and taking leading citizens hostage. He was killed in a battle with British Navy ships commanded by Lieutenant Robert Maynard on November 22, 1718.

▲ *This engraving of Blackbeard comes from* A General History of the Pyrates *by Captain Charles Johnson. The book helped to make some pirates famous.*

AS THEY SAW IT

" 'Damn you for Villains, who are you? And, from whence came you?' The Lieutenant made him Answer, 'You may see by our Colours we are no Pyrates...' Blackbeard took a Glass of Liquor and drank to him with these Words: 'Damnation seize my Soul if I give you Quarters, or take any from you.' In Answer to which, Mr. Maynard told him, That he expected no Quarters from him, nor should he give him any. "

—Lieutenant Robert Maynard of the Royal Navy describes meeting Blackbeard on November 22, 1718.

TRADING WITH CHINA

▲ William Daniell painted this view of the European factories in Canton in around 1800. The flags of each nation fly above each factory.

As more Europeans reached East Asia, the Chinese were determined to control overseas trade. From 1684, the Qing Dynasty allowed foreigners to operate in four cities, including Guangzhou, or Canton, and Macau. Later, from 1757, all foreign traders were confined to an area outside the city walls of Canton. They lived in large complexes of offices, accommodation, and warehouses called factories. Eventually there were thirteen factories, each run by a Chinese merchant on behalf of European, Asian, and American traders.

◀ View of the Foreign Factories *is an 1807 painting of Chinese and European traders during a procession in front of the factories in Canton.*

SOURCE EXPLORED

This painting showing a procession in one of the Canton "factories" in 1807 is thought to be by the Chinese artist Guan Zuolin (also known as Spoilum), who painted in Guangzhou between 1785 and 1810. The thirteen factories were then well established. Each had two or three storeys. The ground floors were used for warehouses, with apartments on the floors above. The buildings were set back 100 yards (91.5 meters) from the river, and the area in front of them was fenced off for foreign merchants. Britain was China's largest Western trading partner. Chinese ceramics and silk were still popular in the West but tea was now China's leading export. The Chinese refused a request from Britain to open access to ports in the north, and Canton retained its dominant position until 1842. After the British defeated China in the First Opium War (1839–1842), the British forced China to open five more ports to foreigners and to hand control of Hong Kong to Britain in the Treaty of Nanking.

AS THEY SAW IT

❝ As the port of Guangzhou is the only one at which outside barbarians are allowed to trade, on no account can they be permitted to wander about to other places in the "Middle Kingdom." The "Son of Heaven," however, whose compassion is as boundless as the ocean, cannot deny to those who are in distress from want of food, through adverse seas and currents, the necessary means of continuing their voyage. When supplied they must no longer loiter, but depart at once. Respect this! ❞

—US sailor William Hunter reports a meeting with Chinese officials who intercepted his ship in 1837.

BRITISH RULE IN INDIA

The fate of the vast Indian subcontinent was decided in a few hours on June 23, 1757. The British had been increasing their presence in India since founding the East India Company in 1601. Now, Robert Clive and a Company army defeated the ruler of Bengal and his French allies in the Battle of Plassey. The British took control of Bengal. Over the next hundred years, their rule expanded to the whole subcontinent. They ruled India until 1947.

▼ *This colored engraving from 1807 shows British army officers startled by a tiger while they hunt wild boar in India.*

SOURCE EXPLORED

This engraving from 1798 by Thomas Daniell shows Government House at Fort St. George in Madras (Chennai) on the Bay of Bengal in India. Founded in 1639, Madras was the first base of the East India Company. Although the Company was a private firm, it ran Bengal and other parts of India more like a government. It set up its own officials, army, and law courts. It also suffered from corruption. After Indian soldiers mutinied against the Company in 1857, the British government took over the powers of the East India Company in 1858 and ran India itself.

▲ Fort St. George was the first British fortress in India. It was renowned for its 150-foot (45.7-meter) teak flagpole, the second-tallest flagpole in the country.

Mountstuart Elphinstone served the East India Company as Governor of Bombay from 1819 to 1827. His enlightened view of Indians contrasted with that of many of his compatriots. He explained the difficulties in 1841:

" Englishmen in India have less opportunity than might be expected of forming opinions of the native character. Even in England few know much of the people beyond their own class, and what they do know they learn from books and newspapers, which do not exist in India. In that country, also, religion and manners put bars to our intimacy with the natives, and limit the number of transactions as well as the free communication of opinions. We know nothing of the interior of families but by report; and have no share in those numerous occurrences of life in which the amiable parts of character are most exhibited. "

CAPTAIN COOK

In 1768, Englishman James Cook sailed on the first of three sea voyages he was to make to the Pacific Ocean. Cook was an expert astronomer and navigator, who used the most up-to-date maritime technology. He took a chronometer, which allowed him to accurately measure longitude, enabling him to pinpoint his exact position. His naval charts set standards for accuracy. His voyages to Tahiti, Australia, New Zealand, the Antarctic Circle, and the Northwest Coast of North America made many contributions to geographical knowledge and the study of the natural sciences.

◄ This portrait of Captain Cook was painted by Nathaniel Dance-Holland in about 1775. It shows the navigator with one of his charts. Cook learned chart-making as a junior officer in the Royal Navy.

In 1772, the French navigator, Julien Marie Crozet, sailed to New Zealand using the maps Cook created:

> " As soon as I obtained information of the voyage of the Englishman, I carefully compared the chart I had prepared for that part of the coast of New Zealand along which we had coasted with that prepared by Captain Cook and his officers. I found it of an exactitude and of a thoroughness of detail which astonished me beyond all powers of expression, and I doubt much whether the charts of our own French coasts are laid down with greater precision. I think therefore that I cannot do better than to lay down our track off New Zealand on the chart prepared by this celebrated English navigator. "

SOURCE EXPLORED

In this drawing—a colored version of an engraving from 1784—Captain Cook and his officers take part in a ceremonial meal with local people in the Sandwich Islands (modern Hawaii). The locals killed and cooked a pig as an offering to the visitors. Despite his efforts to maintain friendly relationships with local people, Cook was killed on his third and final trip to the islands when, on February 14, 1779, he was set upon by islanders on the beach in a dispute about a stolen boat.

▲ This colored engraving is based on an original created by John Webber, an artist who accompanied Cook on his third and final voyage to the Pacific Ocean.

TIMELINE

1405	*The Chinese admiral Zheng He makes his first voyage into the Indian Ocean.*
1416	*Prince Henry of Portugal founds a School of Navigation at Sagres.*
1418	*Portuguese seafarers reach Madeira.*
1431	*Zheng He sets out on his seventh and final voyage to the Indian Ocean.*
1462	*The Portuguese reach Sierra Leone.*
1492	***October 12:** The Italian navigator Christopher Columbus, sailing on behalf of Spain, lands in the Caribbean.*
1497	*The Portuguese sailor Vasco da Gama rounds the southern tip of Africa and sails into the Indian Ocean.*
1498	***May 20:** Da Gama lands in Calicut on the coast of India.*
1503	*Columbus makes the last of his three voyages to the "New World," which he believes is part of the Indies.*
1510	*Spanish traders transport the first African slaves to the islands of the Caribbean.*
1513	*Portuguese traders arrive in the Spice Islands, the Moluccas of Indonesia.*
1519	*Portuguese seafarer Ferdinand Magellan sets sail to find a westerly route to the Spice Islands.*
1521	***April 27:** Magellan dies in a fight between neighboring islands in the Philippines.*
1522	*The survivors of Magellan's expedition return to Portugal, having completed the first circumnavigation of the globe.*
1526	*In India, the Islamic Mughal Dynasty seizes the throne of Delhi, from where they will establish an empire that covers much of the subcontinent.*
1569	*Flemish cartographer Gerardus Mercator invents a method of projecting the globe onto a flat map that sailors can use for practical navigation.*
1581	*The Cossack explorer Yermak Timofeyevich leads the first Russian expedition into Siberia.*

1583	*The Jesuit missionary Matteo Ricci arrives in China.*
1599	*Dutch merchants increase their activities in the Spice Islands, where the Dutch will later establish a virtual monopoly on the spice trade.*
1601	*The Chinese emperor invites Matteo Ricci to Beijing as one of his senior advisers.*
	The British East India Company is established, largely to oversee trade with the Indian subcontinent.
1602	*The Dutch form the Vereenigde Oost-Indische Compagnie (VOC; Dutch East India Company) to control trade with Asia.*
1604	*The VOC establishes its first factory in India.*
1616	*Nathaniel Courthope establishes a short-lived English trading post on Run, one of the Spice Islands.*
1639	*Russian explorers reach the Pacific Ocean.*
	The British East India Company founds its first base in India at Madras on the Bay of Bengal.
1707	*The Mughal Empire in India reaches its largest extent.*
1708	*The first European porcelain is produced at Meissen in Germany.*
1718	*The British pirate Edward Teach, or "Blackbeard," blockades the harbor of Charleston, South Carolina.*
1757	*Foreign traders in China are limited to a small area of "factories" outside the city of Canton (Guangzhou).*
	June 23: *British victory over the ruler of Bengal and his French allies at the Battle of Plassey leads to British control of Bengal, a major step in their eventual conquest of India.*
1768	*British naval officer Captain James Cook makes the first of three voyages of exploration into the Pacific Ocean, reaching Tahiti, New Zealand, and Australia.*
1799	*The VOC is dissolved.*
1842	*At the end of the First Opium War, the British force the defeated Chinese to open more ports to foreign trade under the terms of the Treaty of Nanking.*

GLOSSARY

annexation The seizure of foreign territory by another country or empire.

astrolabe An instrument for making astronomical measurements.

besieged Surrounded and cut off by a hostile force.

cartography The science of making maps and charts.

chronometer A highly accurate watch used to keep time at sea.

circumnavigate To travel around the whole world.

commerce Buying and selling goods, particularly on a large scale.

compass rose A circle divided into segments from which directional bearings can be taken.

dynasty A series of rulers who all come from the same family.

factory Before the nineteenth century, an overseas trading post.

hemisphere Half of the Earth.

Hindu A follower of the ancient religion of India.

idealized Presented as being better than reality.

Islamic Related to Islam, the religion followed by Muslims.

junk An ancient Chinese sailing ship still in use today.

miniature A small, highly detailed, painting.

monopoly The exclusive control of trade in a particular commodity or in a particular place.

monsoon A regular seasonal wind in south and Southeast Asia.

mutinied Rebelled against senior military commanders.

navigation The process of finding one's position and planning a route.

pelt The skin of an animal with the fur still on it.

plantations Large-scale agricultural estates used to grow crops.

porcelain A hard, white, translucent form of ceramic, formed by firing a pure clay at high temperature.

privateers Pirates commissioned by a government to attack ships of a different power.

projection A mathematical method of representing a sphere or part of a sphere on a flat surface.

resources Natural materials that have a useful application.

scurvy A sometimes fatal disease caused by lack of Vitamin C.

skirmish A small-scale clash between military forces.

strait A narrow channel of water connecting two larger seas.

subcontinent A large region that sticks out of a continent; it usually describes the peninsula that includes India, Bangladesh, and Pakistan.

FURTHER INFORMATION

Books

Ariganello, Lisa. *Henry the Navigator: Prince of Portuguese Exploration*. In the Footsteps of Explorers. New York: Crabtree Publishing Co., 2006.

Bailey, Katherine. *Vasco da Gama: Quest for the Spice Trade*. In the Footsteps of Explorers. New York: Crabtree Publishing Co., 2007.

Cooke, Tim. *Blackbeard: A Notorious Pirate in the Caribbean*. Wanted. New York: Gareth Stevens Publishing, 2006.

Hoogenboom, Lynn. *Ferdinand Magellan: A Primary Source Biography*. Primary Source Library of Famous Explorers. New York: PowerKids Press, 2006.

Lace, William W. *Captain James Cook*. Great Explorers. New York: Chelsea House Publishers, 2009.

Sullivan, Laura L. *Blackbeard*. True-Life Pirates. New York: Cavendish Square Publishing, 2015.

Websites

www.ducksters.com/history/ renaissance/age_of_exploration_ and_discovery.php
The Ducksters guide to some of the key breakthroughs of exploration.

www.history.com/shows/mankind- the-story-of-all-of-us/infographics/ age-of-exploration
An introduction to the age of exploration from History.com.

www.ngm.nationalgeographic.com/ ngm/0507/feature2/
A National Geographic article about the Chinese explorer Zheng He.

www.rijksmuseum.nl/en/explore- the-collection/timeline-dutch- history
Pages from the Rijksmuseum about Dutch exploration. Click on the links in the section dated 1595–1640.

Publisher's note to educators and parents: Our editors have carefully reviewed these websites to ensure that they are suitable for students. Many websites change frequently, however, and we cannot guarantee that a site's future contents will continue to meet our high standards of quality and educational value. Be advised that students should be closely supervised whenever they access the Internet.

INDEX